Forex Trading Tips for the Novice

How to Master Online Trading

By: Noel Whitman

I0494191

PUBLISHERS NOTES

Disclaimer

Paperback Edition:

Manufactured in the United States of America

DEDICATION

This book is dedicated to those who work hard to earn extra to support their families and choose to trade Forex. It takes a lot of gumption and resolve to do this the right way.

TABLE OF CONTENTS

CHAPTER 1- FOREX TRADING-THE BASICS

Trading Hours

As Forex trading never closes, more and more people are finding that foreign currency markets are the investments that are best suited to their lifestyle. Forex market hours of operation are 24 hours a day, five days a week. This means that even those who work from nine to five will be able to manage their own accounts from the comfort of their home. If you are looking for an alternative to investing in one of the domestic stock exchanges, you may find that the Forex market is a great fit.

When investors refer to Forex trading, they are talking about making investments in foreign currency. To make an investment, one must simply convert any amount that they wish from their native currency to the foreign currency of their choosing. This can be done at any time, through any number of online and local currency exchange stores. In order to maximize your return on investment, find a country whose currency is undervalued and is comparatively weak against the US dollar. Convert the amount of money that you wish to invest. When the strength of this investment currency improves, change your money back to US dollars, or any other currency of your choosing to yield more than your original investment.

There are brokerage sites online that can help you manage your accounts quickly and effectively. In addition to these sites, one may do this work on his/her own through any currency exchange anywhere. Before setting up an account, one should be aware that the charges associated with carrying out these transactions may vary from place to place, so take some time to research your options.

Though the Forex market trading hours are always open, many experts recommend that any currency exchanges be done during the regular trading hours of your country of choice. Exchange rates can change quickly, and trading during business hours will ensure that the rate at which you are buying is representative of the current financial situation. There is no limit to the amount of time that an investor may hold on to his/her investment, but it is wise to check exchange rates daily to make sure that you are selling at the optimum time. The liberal Forex trading hours have made foreign currency trading more accessible to anyone who is interested in seeking out a new investment opportunity.

Factors That Affect Rates

Now that you are familiar with Forex, you will need to know who moves forex rates. Forex rates do not move for no reason. Forex rates are the same as other economic product prices. Rates are determined by demand and supply. Rates will move till they find an equilibrium price. Economic news could come into the market and affect the demand (buyers) and supply (sellers) and move rates (uptrend or down trend) till buyers and sellers can agree to an equilibrium price. Once an equilibrium price is found, rates will tend to stay stable and consolidate sideways market till another piece of news enters the market and changes the demand and supply equilibrium. Fundamental news, economic data, political events, moral disasters, and market sentiments will affect demand and supply, which will in turn cause forex rates to move.

Understanding Charts

In using charts to analyse currency movement, we tend to use either the bar chart or the candlestick chart. Both convey similar information but are displayed in different ways.

Bar Chart-Bar charts are used to convey, in a graphic form, information of the open, high, low, and close. These are essential for analysing price information.

Each bar represents the open, high, low, and close of price movement observed in a certain time period. This time period is set by the user and can range from one minute to one day, weekly, or monthly. A series of bars will provide a history of price movements, which the chartist uses to analyse and predict price movement.

Candlestick Charting-Candlestick charting displays similar price information as the bar chart, such as the open, high, low, and close. However, the graphical way in which this similar information is displayed differs. Depending on whether the closing price is higher or lower than the opening price, the colour of the candle is different. When the closing price is lower than the opening price, the colour of the body is dark. If the closing price is higher than the opening price, then a light colour body is displayed.

White Candle/Black Candle-I personally like to use candlestick chart. One look at the colour and I know if the candle is an up day or a down day. Using a bar chart, I will need to look at the bar's opening and closing more closely to find out that information.

Choosing An Online Broker

Online brokers are those whom you would call by phone and those that could allow you to just do-it- yourself over the Internet. Many brokers provide both phone services as well as offer an internet trading platform. As most FX brokers offer commission-free trading, we will take that-as a given. We will not consider any broker that charges commission for FX trading.

Which type would be better, a phone-in or internet broker? FX movements are fast at times, especially when you want to trade. Choosing a broker who provides only phone-in trading has its disadvantages. It takes time to dial the broker's phone number, and what happens if the line is engaged? As such, we will eliminate this phone-in only group of brokers. The best option, in my opinion, would be to choose an Internet broker with an online trading platform. In this way, you can trade whenever you spy an opportunity, and immediately seize that opportunity.

If the broker you choose is able to provide charting and news information, it would be an advantage. Cost in terms of the spread would be the most important. In short, the requirements when choosing a broker would be:

- Consistently narrow spread
- Stable and reliable platform
- Charting capability
- News information

CHAPTER 2- STRATEGIES AND INDICATORS

Many new forex traders know that there are specific indicators that they should watch so that they can successfully trade forex. They may pick one particular indicator and rely on it exclusively to nail down a trade and that may work for a while, but then all of a sudden the indicator didn't work! What could have happened? Well, experts have some tips for forex indicators that you might want to consider.

Forex indicators are a great tool, but like most tools, you can't use one in isolation; what good is a hammer without a nail, right? You can't trust a forex signal to be always right, the same thing goes for all forex indicators – good tools are made even better when used appropriately and in tandem with other indicators.

Let's look for example, at one technical indicator, known as the RSI or Relative Strength Index. It's very popular among traders, especially new traders, as it "appears" to have a relatively straightforward interpretation of an overbought (an 80 on the Index) or an oversold (a 20 on the Index) position. Well, if you took some historical analysis of the data, you'd find it isn't as clear-cut as that. In many cases, an oversold or overbought position would only temporarily reverse, with the position becoming even further oversold or overbought.

What experts discovered, and the tip they're willing to share, is that the RSI is more accurate if you consider the position as it moves to and through 50, a good indication that a real trend change is imminent; if RSI moves up through 50, it's an indication of a bull trend, and if it's moving down through 50, it's an indication of a bear trend.

If you combine other indicators with the RSI, your trading could be even more successful. One expert provided this tip: if you're trading short term, go long as RSI moves up through 50 – so long as the Stochastic (or the MACD or EMA) is also moving up through 50.

Technical Indicators

Most forex traders use technical indicators for trading. They found it useful which will give them the busy signals and sell signals but all technical analysis is subject to the user's interpretation. Technical analysts believe that the market's history repeats itself. The psychological nature of the financial market generally, the future is a repetition of the past.

Market prices moves in trends, which persist over a period of time. When in a direction, whether up or down, it will continue to trend. The quote made most frequent "The trend is your friend," or

"Don't fight the market" reflects the fact that the market moves in a trend and is not recommended to trade against a trend, as the odds are you will suffer a loss.

Market price discounts all information. This means that everything that is known at the time is reflected in its price. Therefore all present information or rumour about political, economic, fundamental, psychological or other factor relevant to the price of an asset is already discounted. If any information comes out, the market will immediately factor it into the price, after which the information will no longer be relevant to the process of forecasting.

Trend And Non Trend Indicators

Technical indicators can be classified into two groups. One group is known as the trend-following indicators while the other group is known as the non-trending indicators or oscillators. Non-trending indicators like the RSI and stochastic are useful in a non-trending market.

Trend-following indicators like the moving average follow the trend. They get you into the trend and let you follow the trend until there is a trend change. Then they will signal for you to get out or reverse your position. However, in a non-trending market where price fluctuates in a sideways, horizontal situation, trend following indicators will produce many money-losing signals, which we refer to as whipsaw.

Further on, we will take a look at the moving average, which is a trend following indicator. MACD can be considered a trend following indicator as it is actually the difference between two exponential moving averages. However, this indicator also has some oscillator properties, with the way the MACD Line oscillates between the zero line and the signals generated by the zero line crossover.

Both RSI and stochastic are oscillators, and they work well in a non-trending market condition. The Bollinger band can be used on its own without other technical indicators. Many traders in FX trading use these few indicators mentioned, which are chosen from the two different groups of technical indicators.

On Balance Volume

Markets tend to top and bottom with spikes in trading volume. These volume spikes are caused by an influx of orders by traders acting on news, reports, recommendations by advisors, and/or large buying or selling by commercial interests. Trading volume is important because it often can alert you to market tops and bottoms. The actual final volume of contracts traded at any given price is generally unavailable to the public until after the trading session. Estimates are possible to obtain, but this is a time-consuming process and difficult to maintain on a regular basis. The short-term trader is, therefore, limited in his or her access to, and use of, volume figures. Tic volume provides a good substitute for actual contract volume. Tic volume measures the number of price changes rather than the actual number of contracts traded. Tic volume is a cumulative total of price changes over a given period of time. Tic volume moves up and down with increases and decreases in activity.

The Value Of Tic Volume

Tic volume is valuable to the short-term trader for several reasons:

- It allows one to determine when and where major activity is taking place.

- It allows one to gauge whether the activity was primarily selling pressure or buying pressure.
- It can serve as a technical indicator on its own.
- It can serve as a confirming indicator when used with other signals.

Tic volume can help you spot price levels at which significant activity took place in the past, and are likely to occur again in the future.

Basic Characteristics Of Tic Volume

Another way to use tic volume is to monitor tic volume trends in relation to price trends. Remember as a rule of thumb that expanding tic volume on the downside is a bearish indication, and contracting tic volume on the downside indicates that the downtrend should soon end. On the upside, expanding tic volume indicates a rally, and contracting tic volume suggests that the rally is likely to end soon.

It should be remembered that volume often contracts on price declines because many traders are afraid of the short side. This is why the OBV/price relationships mentioned earlier are not observed easily on the volume and price data. There is, however, another way to look at OBV tic that makes its value more readily discernible—the OBV tic trendline.

OBV Tic Trendline

Another way to look at tic volume in relation to price is to simply monitor trendline penetrations of OBV tic. As comical as it may sound, much depends upon how thin or thick the lines are drawn. Yet, there are ways in which trendline analysis can be operationalized, but I must leave this task to those willing to undertake it. There are several additional aspects of OBV that can be employed in a short-term trading program.

Divergence And Tic Volume

"Divergence" is defined as "an indicator and price moving in different directions." Basically, the use of divergence and tic volume takes two forms:

- When price makes a new high for a given time frame, but the new high is not confirmed by a tic indicator high, divergence is negative, suggesting that a decline in price is likely.
- When price makes a new low for a given time period but tic indicator fails to make a new low, divergence is positive, suggesting that an up move in price is likely.

OBV is another example of a market technique as opposed to a trading system. On balance volume is an important concept which should be developed further by those inclined to do so. Consider also the possibility of using second order derivatives of OBV. In other words, consider using an RSI indicator of OBV as a second order technical indicator of on balance volume. I have done some preliminary work in this direction which seems to be very promising.

Chapter 3- Money Management

Preserving Your Capital

Forex trading is a high leverage game so preserving capital is the key to success in trading. You just have to put up US$2000 but you are trading US$100,000 in value. The deposit amount is equivalent to just 200 pips movement in EUR/USD. One wrong move and that would be enough to wipe out-your-entire capital. For the Euro to move 200 pips in a couple of days is not uncommon. As the daily range of the Euro is around 100 pips a day, a single day of movement can set you back by US$1000. That would mean 50% of your capital would be burnt off in just a single day. In another couple of days, all your capital could be wiped off. With such high leverage involved in forex trading, it is important for you to be disciplined. If you do not use good money management by locking in your profits and cutting your losses, you may wipe out your capital easily. Maintain your trading discipline and keep your losses small. You must know how to be a good fund manager.

Most of the new traders will have the temptation to go in the market quickly and want to make money right away, but unfortunately most do not make money. So making no profit and preserving your investment capital is better than losing your capital. Be clear with your direction and wait until the right time to enter your trade. Patience and discipline are the keys to ensure your capital is preserved and the experience that you gained will help you to make profit another day.

The more you lose, the more you will take effort and time to get back to where you started from: for example making 10% return from $10000 will generate you $1000 profit but if you have lost half of your capital then you left with $5000. So if you make same 10% return out of $5000, you only make $500 and you have to double your effort or profit to make same $1000.

Forex Trading Tips

Good money management must have two golden rules, a) avoid losing money b) avoid missing profit opportunities. As a new trader, you should focus on more conservative strategy in order to build up the capital to trade more aggressively in the future. Trader 'A' took the position but it never went his direction so he decided to hold it so he may end up holding for a few days or up to a week. On the other hand, Trader B took the same position but knowing that the market was not going his way, he decided to close the position at a small loss(2%) the he took another position later with a profit of 30% so the net profit of his trade was 28%. Because of his decision to cut loss, he made higher percentage of profit which made his account grow bigger at the end of the day.

Remember, your main focus is to preserve your capital investment and this will protect you from running of money to trade in the futures. Trading is all about survival game.

Drawdown And Money Management

As a good trader must have good money management principles. We may take a look at how crucial money management is and what are the consequences of not having "money management rules." let see this example:

You have $10,000 in your account and you lose $5,000. What percentage of your capital have you lost? It is 50%. Now, what percentage of that $5,000 capital do you have to make so that you will get back to your original $10,000? It is no longer 50%. You have to double up your return which is 100% to get back to your original $10,000. This is called drawdown. For this case, we would have a 50% drawdown.

From this simple illustration, it is clear that it is very easy to lose money but you have to work harder to make it back. In the worst case scenario, if we lose 5, 6, or even 10 trades continuously. We may face "Margin Call" when we do not use good money management rules.

In trading, we must have a sound trading system. If a trading system that can give us 80% profitable trades, it is considered a very good system. However, with this trading system, does it mean for every 50 trades you place, you will win 40 out of every 50?

The answer is "not really." because we do not know which 40 out of these 50 trades will be winners. One trader may lose the first 10 trades continuously and only win the balance 40. This is still considering an 80% profitable system, but the key question is this: "Would this trader still preserve his/her capital if he/she has lost 10 trades in a row?" You can see why money management is so important. Although the trading system is good he/she may eventually lose everything if he does not practice good money management rules.

In order to be a good trader we must only risk a very small percentage of our capital in every single trade so that we can still survive even when we are in our losing streak. Remember that, trading is a journey or survival game, if we apply strict money management rules, we will become the winner in the long term. Next You will learn about risk management, which is another means of preserving protecting and preserving your capital.

CHAPTER 4- RISK MANAGEMENT

Let's tackle risk management first. Simply stated, you must always apply strong risk management principles when trading. Indeed, it is the most important success factor as experienced traders and certainly successful traders know. There is a reason for this. There is no method on the face of the earth that wins every trade. It is simply impossible, and it is why you must pay attention first and foremost to risk. Here is an example. If you have a winning method that wins 66% on the average and has a probability of three successive losing trades 4% of the time, here is what the 66% winning trades method would yield: three successive losing trades 4% of the time. Even with a good method like that, you will have three losing trades.

If you risk 33% of your initial capital on each trade, of course you will eventually be wiped out. This is an extreme example, but it makes the point that you can have a great method and with poor risk management wipe out your account.

There are many ways and formulas to determine what the supposedly optimal level of risk is that you should incur on each and every trade. I have found that, once again, simple is better. If you do not have a simple rule, you will probably not follow it, and you could get yourself into a lot of trouble.

Limiting Your Risk

Here is the simple rule. It is not just simple, but it is very powerful and it works just fine. Risk no more than 2% of your trading account on each trade. You could risk up to 5% for accounts under $5,000 for a more aggressive trader. Risk means the amount you are willing to lose, not the amount applied to make the trade. Let's take an example.

For a $5,000 account, by risking 2% you would risk no more than $100 per trade. If on the next trade you bought too many lots and lost $100, your account balance would be $4,900, limiting your risk on the next trade to 2% of $4,900 or $98. You are not going to risk more on the next trade; you are going to risk less. By limiting your risk to 2% of each trade using the first example (where you lost three in a row and risked 33% on each trade and got wiped out), by risking 2% of your account now you would only be down $294 after three losing trades in a row to $4,700 and change. That is quite a difference. You are still in the game, and no major damage has been done. You are now in position to experience some winning trades.

If you lose three in a row with a method that gives you an edge, there will be reversion to the mean. This means there are profitable trades coming, and it could be you would get five in a row of those. You would not only make up for your losses, but also you would be well ahead. However, you have to be in the game for this to happen.

You lose three in a row, but on the other hand, as you pile up winning trades and your account grows, you can risk up to 2% of the growing account balance. Only as your account grows would you risk more dollars per trade. It is still no more than 2% of your account balance, but as your account grows, you can risk more dollars. As it shrinks, if you lose a trade or two, you risk less.

This is the exact opposite of what a lot of traders do. If they lose one or two, they think they have to get it all back on the next trade, and they risk too much on the next trade. You should not do that.

Position Size In Forex

Now we will discuss position size. Let's take an example. For a $5,000 account, by risking 2% you plan to lose no more than $100 on the trade or 2% of $5,000. If the next trade risked 20 pips per mini lot between the entry price and your stop, you would be risking $20 per mini lot. This is one dollar per pip. Determine your maximum position size by dividing the amount of your account being risked by the per-lot risk in the trade. In this example, it is $100 being risked divided by the per-lot risk, $20, and that equals five mini lots. This is the maximum number of mini lots you could trade for that example. You are risking 20 pips, and if you lost, you would lose $20. Five mini lots equal $100 which is 2% of your account size. This is how you determine your position size. It is very simple. Always round down. If it does not come out to an even number of lots, round down and risk.

This way you always know the maximum number of lots to put on any one trade. Remember, this does not mean that you must trade the maximum allowed; it is just the maximum. You can trade less. When we consider this example, trading only two mini lots would risk less than 1% of your account. This would be just fine.

Number Of Positions In Forex

Let's talk now about the number of positions you have open at any point in time. In day trading up to 30-minute bars, I believe it is best to have only one trade open at a time. If you are trading hourly or greater time frames, I think you could have up to two trades open at one time, and it would be manageable.

You can certainly have more open positions than this, but the key here is to keep it simple. You do not want to create unnecessary stress by overtrading. There is plenty of opportunity; there is no need to do that.

As you gain experience, you will be able to determine your own personal comfort level regarding which time frames and the amount of trading you want to do.

Increasing Winning Ratio

In forex trading, the chance of success when you take a position is 50:50. You will either make money or you lose money on your position. It is this simple. If you can achieve a success rate of 50% on your trade, you will break-even as there is no commission cost in forex trading. If you can achieve a 70% success rate in your trading, you should be making money. It is based on the assumption that every loser is the same as every winner.

It is important you do not trade "freestyle". You do not trade simply because you feel like trading. You need to follow guidelines and methodology in your trading. When there is nothing to trade on, you should not trade. When your favourite patterns or indicators appear, then you should enter a trade.

That does not mean there are no other winning formulas left. You could do your own research and maybe come up with a better tool that can help you in trading but it is better to learn from a good trader. There are many indicator combinations possible. It is up to your imagination to combine the vast array of indicators. But before you actually commit your hard-earned money to trade using them, it is best you test those indicators with historical data or a demo setup.

Increasing Your Win/Loss Ratio

The second step towards becoming a successful forex trader is to increase your profitability per trade. This is where your risk/reward and trade management comes in. To be successful, you will need to have a risk to reward ratio of one to two. That means you need to make twice the amount of your losses. For every position you enter, if your stop loss is limited to 30 pips, your take profit must be 60 pips. That will give you a risk to reward ratio of one to two. If you were to lose 30 pips on every trade and if your winners are 60 pips, based on a 50% success rate, you should be making 150 pips on every ten trades. If you have a 70% winning ratio, that would be 330 pips earned on every ten trades. This is the game plan necessary for trading success.

There is no slippage for a stop loss, as most online brokers will fill your stop loss at the exact price where you place your stop loss order. However, when news or economic data is being announced, there will be slippages, as brokers cannot guarantee fills at the exact price due to unusual fast rate movements.

Even if your trading is not that good, as long as you have good trading discipline, you can still make money. If you have only four winners out of ten and If you have a win to loss ratio of two is to one, you can still make money from forex. You do not need to know much about technical analysis or fundamental news to be right 50% of the time. It is not wrong to say trading discipline is more important than your methodology or trading system. If you have a winning system or methodology but no discipline, you can still be wiped out of your capital with just a single big losing trade.

CHAPTER 5- SHORT-TERM TRADERS VS. LONG-TERM TRADERS

Rules For Short Term Trader

The strategy of the short-term trader is distinctly different from that of the intermediate or long-term trader. The long-term trader seeks to establish a position at or near major turning points, in expectation of a fairly long ride in the expected direction; the day trader and the short-term trader rarely considers such endeavors. Rather, the short- term trader looks primarily for opportunities within the existing trend. The behavior of the short-term trader and the long-term trader is similar to the hunting strategies of the lion and the vulture.

Unless exceptionally hungry, the lion hunts big game. Days and days may pass before the opportunity for a big kill presents itself, but when it does, the lion moves in stealthily, carefully, with forethought and cunning. Once the lion has its teeth in its prey, it will not relent: it will fight, risking self-injury in its efforts to win the large prize. If the prey escapes, the lion has invested no more than effort and, perhaps, a bit of its hide. If it is cautious, the lion will not suffer much pain in executing its strikes, which, though few and far between, are handsomely rewarding. And so it is with the long-term trader.

The vulture seeks opportunities created by the misfortune of others. Rather than going after living, large prey—which requires a tremendous amount of effort and considerable risk—the vulture looks only for many small opportunities that are relatively free of danger; its only competition comes from other vultures seeking the same opportunities. As basic as this analogy may seem, I think it strikes home. The short-term trader must be a vulture, looking for opportunities that present limited risk as well as the potential for a quick reward. Because of his/her very nature, the short-term trader is not concerned with big prey, or with what the competition (i.e., the long-term trader) is doing at any given point in time. It is entirely possible for both kinds of traders to exist without competing with each other, as do the lion and the vulture. An opportunity for the lion may also prove ultimately to be an opportunity for the vulture. By reacting to living prey the vulture can alert the lion to a possible opportunity. The lion may take the big risk and fell the prey, leaving the remains for the vulture.

Since the short-term trader and long-term trader seek different types of opportunities, they can work well in the same environment. A long-term trader may sell to a short-term trader, and vice versa. Each creates opportunities for the other. At times, both may compete for the same opportunity, but with different expectations.

In order to take effective advantage of short-term opportunities, the trader must keep in mind a number of general rules and principles about short-term trading. The suggestions that follow deserve the consideration of anyone and everyone who wishes to trade in short- term time frames.

Decide On Your Time Frame

Determine whether you plan to be a day trader or whether you are willing to carry positions for up to five days. By knowing your time orientation in advance you will know how to act within the time frame. A day trader will be out of all positions by the end of each day. This means that he or she will need to respond more quickly to market opportunities during the day. I don't believe it is a good idea to enter the market in one time frame with certain expectations and then to change those expectations in order to exit the market from another time frame. It is important to determine whether you will be a day trader or another type of short-term trader. Although the techniques of entry may be similar, techniques and expectations for exit are not.

As a Short-Term Trader Your Approach Primarily Will Be:

Technical

Reports, fundamentals, announcements, and news will provide temporary shifts in market trends that, with effective technical tools, you will be able to take advantage of for the purpose of entry and exit on your short-term trades. A majority of your trading should be on technical signals.

Types Of Orders

Many of your orders will be market orders. Learn to use market orders. Don't hesitate to enter or exit at the market, particularly if you are a day trader. Although some of the methods in this book require price orders, do not be afraid to enter or exit at the market when necessary.

Don't Ride Losses

Don't ride losses beyond your originally intended point. Make certain that you enter and exit according to your system as often as you can, sticking to your rules as much as possible.

Mechanical Trading vs. "Artistic" Trading

While there is much to be said in favor of a totally mechanical system, there are times when science must give way to art. Try to establish the validity of your market intuition; determine when it can be trusted. Being overly rigid is not always in your best interest.

Don't Be Afraid To Enter On Reactions Within An Existing Trend

Many of the techniques described in this book are based on trend reactions. When reactions within the trend occur, traders often believe that the trend has ended and that further trades can't be justified. In a good uptrend or downtrend, though, reactions are usually quite reliable for entry purposes. You must learn to overcome the fear of entering the market, and you must avoid second-guessing the system. The odds are clearly in your favor when you enter on trend reactions.

Think For Yourself

Don't rely too much on information from outside sources. Take the systems, methods, and ideas to which you have been exposed and integrate them into an approach that makes sense to you and gives you results. Develop your own style, methods, and rules.

Don't Attempt To Trade By Long Distance

As a short-term trader, you must be in touch with the markets quite frequently. It is unwise to trade with insufficient information or while you are out of touch with the market. I know many a trader who has attempted this and has paid a dear price indeed.

Do Your Homework

Whatever combination of techniques or system you ultimately arrive at, make certain that you keep your work up to date. If your work is not up to date, don't trade.

Trade Frequently, But Not Just For The Sake Of Trading

Forex Trading Tips

The best way to maximize capital from day trading or short-term trading is to trade frequently. This keeps your capital working. But you must be careful not to create trades or signals where none exist. To trade simply for the sake of trading is ultimately a losing proposition.

Be Aggressive

After you have traded with a particular system or method for a while you'll develop a sense for it that will alert you to the best opportunities—when you see these you'll recognize them, and your response should be an aggressive one. Follow the major trend of the market, adding to positions when you can, thereby maximizing your profit from such moves.

Understand Market Behavior

There are many different theories about the marketplace, each with its own rules and explanations. Understand how your system works: what it is saying about the marketplace and what it is saying about each trade you make. Understanding how a system works can tell you a great deal about the nature of the market at any given point in time.

Trade Active Markets Only

Short-term and day traders have minimal price and time advantage in inactive markets. They need good volume for entry and exit, and good prices swings to make entry and exit worthwhile.

There are many other things that the short-term trader will need to know. They can be learned only from experience. Because the character of the market changes with time, it is impossible to declare without reservation that all of these suggestions will continue to serve you many years. As an individual speculator, the most important thing that you can do is understand the concepts of the market and the nature of your relationship to the market. Then you will be able to change with the market, instead of fighting change in the market.

CHAPTER 6- FOREX TRADING-TRADING PSYCHOLOGY

In order to be successful in trading you must not bring your bad habits and emotion to the market. Having good habits and managing your emotion well is like acquiring the best helmet possible to protect you from failure. Your mindset is the captain of your destiny.

Most traders agreed that more than 80% of the price movement is due to human psychology that is greed and fear emotions. Because of these emotions, sometimes price move irrationally. If a trader cannot control his emotions, trading will be too costly and can wipe out the capital easily. Most traders think that strategy is the most important aspect in trading but for professional traders understanding that to be a successful trader one must conquers his/her emotions or so called trading psychology. They know greed and fear are the greatest enemies in trading, so they are not afraid of losing and are not greed, in any trades.

A new trader is fearful of losing so he/she never admits his/her fault and usually refuses to cut losses and some will add position to a losing trade. Some fear missing out on the big move opportunities so they take position without following the trading plan and usually they make the wrong decisions, but sometimes they may profit from not following the rules. This is the most expensive profit trade that they have ever made. Usually, they will lock in profit too fast as they are afraid of the market taking the profit away. On the other hand, because of greed they will never be satisfied with whatever they make and will always want more and sometimes they will hold too long until they turn profit trade to losing trade.

Most traders lose money in the market because they trade for excitement and fun. They do not know the purpose of trading; they do not have goals in mind. If you know the purpose, you may make a living or even make a fortune in forex trading. They think they want to make profit out of the market but subconsciously they just trade for excitement and fun. It is just like gambling, most people lose money in casinos but there are still many people who want to gamble in casinos. We must see trading as a business, if we can make a profit in that trade only we take position or else just stay cool. Preserving your capital is more important than winning trades.

Professional traders always have a clear goal. They only trade when they are calm, cool and focused. They also have a right and abundance mindset, focus on winning trades. They make decisions based on their plan but not emotions. That is why they are the winners in the market and they are also the active losers which mean they admit wrong and cut loss without hesitation. They respect the market and believe the market is always right so never revenge the market. Blaming the market is shifting responsibility to the market. They do not attach greed, fear and hope emotions in their trading decisions.

We are responsible for our winning or losing trades. Whenever we make a losing trade or mistake, we must learn from it, understand it and accept it. A good trader knows his/her risk tolerance level. They know losing is part of trading; trading is a journey not destination. Mistakes are painful when they happen, but years later, collection is called experience, which lead to success. A professional trader always visualizes himself as a successful trader whenever he/she trades, this is called self-image. You can learn more about visualization in Psycho-Cybernetics by Dr.Maxwell Maltz. To be a successful trader, you must plan your trade and trade your plan. Below are some tips on how to become a successful trader.

<u>Follow Rules Consistently</u>

Successful traders always follow the trading rules and the proven trading system consistently. By following the rules, they have consistent good trading results. Rules always help them to structure the trading, help them to avoid mental mistakes. The only way to be a good trader is to follow the rules as they are 100% responsible for their results. Successful traders set their own trading rules and update it as often as they can. Mostly, new traders will not follow the rules as they afraid of missing out on a good trade. If you follow the rules and make the right decisions you will be successful in trading in one day.

Have A Trading Plan

Successful traders have a proven and structured trading plan before they enter the market. With a clear trading plan they know what the entry price is and when to exit; they know their profit target and risk level in advance. By following the trading plan, they know what to do when the market goes against them or in their favour. This will help them to get rid of the emotion of greed and fear; they will not be affected by the fluctuation of the price movement. A good written trading plan will increase your probabilities in your winning trade. With a trading plan, trading becomes stress-free and easy.

Have A Trading Journal

Experienced traders are always keeping their trading journal by recording their winning and losing trades. They record their mistakes, this is more important. It is okay to make mistakes because losing is part of trading but you must learn something from the mistakes, if you don't record them then you are bound to repeat them. Keeping a trading journal make you become an experienced trader.

Use A Stop Loss

Even when you follow the trading rules you may still face some losing trades but with the stop loss order you will preserve your capital and limit your loss. Most importantly, it will help you manage your emotion well. It is just like a safety net, when the market is against you, you will be out automatically with the calculated minimum loss. Normally a good trader will place their stop loss not more than 5 percent of their capital. By placing stop loss, you have automated your trades and will not let your emotion make you panic. Do not use mental stop loss; you will hesitate when the market is against you. Using a stop loss, will prevent you from making emotional decisions and remember never remove your stop order no matter what is the market conditions.

Automated Profit With A Target Profit

Experienced traders do not watch the market for several hours each day. They calculate their profit and set the target profit in advance so that their position will be liquidated automatically without them getting emotionally involved. You only need to monitor your trade for a short period of time and may change your order when it is necessary. Then just switch off your computer. With the Target Profit order, you are no longer attaching to emotion and so make money while you are asleep. You may key in One Cancel Other (OCO) order means Stop Loss and Target profit at the same time.

Discipline

Professional traders always abide by their trading rules and are cautious even after sequential gains. Smart traders plan their trades before going in the market and trade only with their plan. For example, they never trade without stop loss orders and never risk more than 5% of their capital. They will follow and stick to rules though they tempt to violate it. Being disciplined will remove you from opinions and emotion from others. Discipline is the key to succeed in forex trading.

Be 100% Responsible

Every successful trader is responsible for his/her results and never blames the market. Even if he/she make mistake, he/she admits it and will review his/her trades and never repeat it. Successful traders value mistakes as they are the valuable lessons for success. They forgive themselves for the losing trades, no regret, no remorse or guilt in their mind. They respect the market all the time and always act in their own best interest. To improve yourself to be a good trader, you must fully responsible for your own results.

Have A Balanced Life

Why so many people love trading is because trading will lead us to financial independence, give us time and freedom so that we can spend more quality time with our family members. Successful traders never try to control the market; they seem to be very confident and relaxed though trading is quite stressful. Take a break or holiday occasionally, recharge your battery, enjoy your life and gain some new perspective. You have to pamper your inner child so that your subconscious mind will be provoked to excel in the future. Having a balanced life will improve your results.

Positive Self-Image

Self-image controls everything in our lives because what we believe will be conceived. It is a picture of us in our mind. The best traders will see themselves vividly as successful traders in their own minds. They have no doubt in their trading system and have full confidence in themselves. They believe they deserve making a lot of money in forex trading. If they do not have this positive self-image they tend to give back their money back to the market in the subconscious mind though they have made it. The positive self-image is more powerful and stronger than any willpower. If you face problems in trading or a losing streak all the time, then you must check your self-belief system about trading. Do you have confidence in yourself? Do you focus on losing trades all the time? Do you deserve to make money from the market quickly? Do you blame yourself when you make a losing trade? You must change your view of yourself so you will deserve making fast money in trading.

- Follow the trading plan.
- Do not chase after the market, let the market come to you.
- Be Patient.
- Must learn from mistakes.
- Trade only with chart not emotion.
- Trade only with stop order.
- Do not overtrade.
- Visualize before you trade.
- Read trading rules before you trade.
- Always be happy with your profit.
- Never trade for excitement, have reasons before you enter your order.
- Have no emotion involved while you are trading.
- Do not repeat breaking the "rules breaking" winning trade.
- Do not stare on the screen to find any set up trade.
- Do not revenge over losing trade.
- Switch off your computer after placing your trade.
- Pay yourself consistently.
- Trade with a clear mind and good mood.
- Do not change your stop loss and target profit order.
- If you are not sure, do not trade.
- Maintain a trading journal.
- Trade with consistent lot size unless your capital increased by 25%.
- Do not add losing trades to your position.
- Do not expose your risk more than 5% of your capital.
- Learn to cut your loss.
- Admit wrong and do not blame the market.
- Do not trade against the trend, trade with the trend.
- Do not trade too many pairs of currency at once.

Many of the maladies that tend to affect short-term traders are conditioned responses (unconsciously learned) to market behaviour. Because traders have engaged in trading for such a long time, the stimulus of the marketplace elicits the response of wanting to trade. This response can occur even in the absence of trading signals. The mere act of watching the market is often enough to arouse the trading response in many traders. Such behaviour provides a textbook case of operant conditioning and stimulus generalization, concepts defined and discussed by B. F. Skinner in his classic works on the conditioning of organisms. Essentially, Skinner's work demonstrated that much of our behaviour is learned, or conditioned, voluntarily and subtly, by those around us, from our environment, and from our experiences. An understanding of the work of such psychological learning theorists as Skinner, Hull, Tolman, Pavlov, and others, will help you understand how we are conditioned by the stimulus of the market place to respond in a certain way. Although much of their work was done with laboratory animals, many findings of the learning theorists have been clearly and unequivocally demonstrated to apply to humans as well. It is entirely possible that rats and pigeons are better learners than humans, but I am not interested in debating the applicability of results from animal studies to the behaviour of human beings—I know that they are applicable in one sense or another. Conditioning (otherwise known as learning) can result in the development of faulty behaviour patterns. The need to trade is a conditioned response that occurs as a function of the unconscious learning process. Knowing you are susceptible to such behaviour and being able to recognize it, will allow you to stop it before it starts, or at least stop it shortly after its onset.

The Inability To Stick To Your Plans

Forex Trading Tips

The most common trading errors committed by those involved in short-term trading is the inability to stay with a plan, program, system or method. This is so common a problem, in fact, that an entire book could be written about it. Without entering into a lengthy explanation of this issue, here are a few things to consider if you are having difficulty staying with your method or system:

Do You Really Have Confidence In Yourself?

If you lack the conviction that you can do well in the markets, you will be prone to inconsistencies in your trading decisions. Such inconsistencies will not only limit your ability to stay with a given system or method—they will also manifest themselves in a constant need to second-guess or modify the specific dictates of your trading system. Another manifestation will be the inability to ride winners and close out losers. All in all, the entire potential of your trading approach could be considerably diminished if you fail to have a positive attitude about your abilities.

Do You Have Confidence In Your Trading System?

Some trading systems naturally inspire confidence, either in oneself or in one's system. But if you lack confidence in your system or method, you will be susceptible to the same inconsistent and unprofitable behaviours described earlier. Furthermore, you also will be vulnerable to the error of mixing your system with the input of other systems, and market behaviours that are not systematic. The result will be no system at all. One way to build confidence in your system or method is to study its performance over a fairly lengthy period of time. Learn how your system works in good times and in bad. Learn how the system has behaved in bull markets, bear markets, and sideways markets. Although it is certainly true that the historical performance of any trading approach does not guarantee its present or future performance, there is some confidence to be gained from its record, particularly if it has a long history. If you can't have confidence in the system and if the system can't instil confidence in you, drop it and find something new.

Too Much Information

Many traders are influenced by a steady influx of information from outside sources such as associates, brokers, newspapers, newsletters, relatives, and so on. Some traders are unable to minimize the influence of external information and frequently react to it by misinterpreting or mishandling their trading approach. The best way for most traders to deal with this type of input is to shut it off. If you find, upon review, that a good many of your losses are due to unwarranted reliance upon external information, then by all means take steps to prevent your exposure to it.

ABOUT THE AUTHOR

Noel Whitman was never a risk taker. He was an extremely methodical individual that loved to take things one step at a time and he always had a backup plan. It was not strange then that when Forex trading started to become a popular option for many to earn extra that he opted to simply watch and learn for a while before trying it out for himself.

It was a bit challenging at first but Noel stuck to the task and after a while it all started to become easier as he understood the Forex platform some more.